Mouthful of Bees

Shannon Quinn

Mansfield Press

Library and Archives Canada Cataloguing in Publication

Title: Mouthful of bees / Shannon Quinn.
Names: Quinn, Shannon, 1971- author.
Description: Poems.
Identifiers: Canadiana 20210343826 | ISBN 9781771262712 (softcover)
Classification: LCC PS8633.U577 M68 2021 | DDC C811/.6—dc23

Cover Images: Shutterstock
Typesetting & Cover Design: Denis De Klerck

The publication of *Mouthful of Bees* has been generously supported by
the Canada Council for the Arts and the Ontario Arts Council.

Mansfield Press Inc.
25 Mansfield Avenue, Toronto, Ontario, Canada M6J 2A9
Publisher: Denis De Klerck
www.mansfieldpress.net

The crisis consists precisely in the fact that the old is dying
and the young cannot be born;
in this interregnum a great variety of morbid symptoms appear.

Antonio Gramsci
(1891-1937)

A Collection in Six Sequences and One Myth

Prologue

Madness & Recovery

The Monster's Been Made

Life Now

Monuments

The Book of Blue Hurts

Mythos
Fragments from the Biophilia Codex

Prologue

SONG TO TURN A BODY HOME

What is a human soul but a claw pointing back to the forest?
Don Domanski

I'd like to learn to be a person with you in grey light
where everything that is possible can begin:

a day to throw ourselves in front of moving vehicles
survive every time

an afternoon where trees stretch out
in the drunkest part of sun

an early hour for rabbits to kick cages, dance through snares
as they paint illuminated manuscripts inside us:
the story of humans, how surprised we were to be temporary.

When you've had enough, tell me.

All we need is a little extra morphine and an open window
to call your rabbits in from the woods.
Even now with our meaning too young for us
they start their chant:

it's safe, it's safe

yes it hurts

but it's safe.

ONTARIO LAKESHORE ASYLUM

Dear Soft Listening Novice,
You are too late for the light and don't know nearly enough, but stay.
All blessings are welcome here.
Have you come to transcribe our names?
Harvest our songs? Promise to play them from an open window
on a summer night, so that even with our untended graves, they can
never say we were a mystery.

THE PACK ANIMAL TAROT

Who are you today? Pick. I've printed them all on cards.
What did you get? Mother of Mysterious Births?
Solar Horse? Wolf with Silver Teeth?

Did you pick one that scares you?

Nobody wants to be Contagion or Ritual Sacrifice.

This is my fifth day in a row as Wolf with Silver Teeth.
Yesterday was a massacre.
I'm trying to be mindful about my instincts.

I count to ten. Exhale. I hear the tired heart of my cat,
smell his sour breath. We won't see September together. Instinct.

Child? Did you pull the Child? We all want that one
to be able to find a lap and whisper *please make it stop.*
But this is the age of Pack Animal Democracy—we come together
only to splinter.

Please make my heart bigger today so that when I run at the edge
of the pack,
I don't use my teeth just because I like how it feels.

If I slow myself down, linger, it almost feels like forgiveness.

A BEAUTIFUL MATH

In the Holy Week of the Pandemic all of our dead resurrect after three days. It's uncomfortable. They don't have the Jesus-Lilac-Smell as advertised. Even after resurrection there is a hierarchy of bodies. We open our arms to those plumped with formaldehyde. We fear the wandering unclaimed ones. We owe them something. We think we can't pay. We need this lie. The cremated also resurrect (I've buried the lead). Living as ash, they quiver in our presence. They no longer understand our binary thinking. They cry sanctuary in the wind. Marvel at the beauty of one. Linger by the corners of infestation. Their own spatter along the walls a model for how infectious droplets travel through air. It's a beautiful math. But this is not my first plague. What I wouldn't give to be on a crowded dance floor, covered in ash, spines ululating: Promise   Defy   Endure

LAST BOY ASTRONAUT

You shiver in your sister's nightgown.
You stand in the middle of the road.
You love animals, space exploration.
Your mother falls asleep on top of you.
Your father writes cheques to your missing sister.
Another Kennedy is shot.
You look up to see there are no adults in the room.

   Wait. Go back.

You shiver in your sister's nightgown, dream
of Sputnik's soft landing by the cottage dock.

You straddle the rail in the middle of the street
plastic sheriff's badge pinned to your chest
toy gun cocked to arrest the oncoming streetcar.

You have a dog named Peterbelle, a cat named Drumcliffe.

This will be exhausting but you will work
your entire life to keep these memories

   separate, clean & true.

THUNDER IN OUR FENCED YARD

I watch starlings ungather
take flight, wheeling insides
hollow bones
full of the questions mom asks:

did you touch me?
do I want to pray?
wrong questions

we heard you might be heading east
maybe the bus station in Halifax or Fredericton

wherever you are   call home?

TRANSMISSION

It's a room next to the one I'm in, not unfamiliar but unexpected, a simple truth and an expansive transition. It's lights in the brain blinking out, like staring at the filament in an old lightbulb or like watching a snake warm her blood in the sun (surprised I've never considered this, but look, there she is, and of course). It's like finally understanding the five figures in blue linen from my dreams *are* my dreams moving away from me and everyone is fine, we are all fine and yes, those five figures might be my own brothers and sisters but still, everyone is fine. Someone will always light a candle. This is how we remember breath along with every other point of transmission: a link within a link within a link to the delicately diminished. It's the inhalation, the wonder at the thought; what fine work here.

THE SCARS TO PROVE IT

Faith is a dry, cracked place for you.
Drink this cup of water.
Ring your body like a bell.

Make your own feast day.
Ring your body for the rabbit-hearted god
who loved you when you were ten.

The High Church was hard on you:
small precise cuts along back of thigh,
hidden bottles & fingers down the throat.

That's over now.
Ring your body like a bell. Pray in peace.
The knife & the sacrifice don't live here anymore.

WE MEET IN THE WATER, THIS MUCH IS TRUE

devotion can starve a body, leave
it with a handful of pixels to see by

ask the salmon, throwing themselves
upstream, their cellular imperative
driving them home

ask the porchlight from our old house
as it flashes then pops
(tungsten hiss of joy-pitted obsolescence)

mid-spirit, you have a spine of cracked
light & a fresh mouth to bray with
as your analogue god wraps his arms
around your ankles

so drink that river dry, eat the porchlight, leave bread
for the birds, an envelope for the church

celebrate
this is the year of the great conjunction
look down
it's only mud around your feet
meet your new self
a bright stuttering knife

soul attached by one phosphor thread

EQUANIMITY

walk to the sea
flutter cupped in hand
pass over rabbit warren
fear shoots up through feet

bless the dogs that hunt

arrive at sea
uncup your hands
say goodbye

this one kept to the woods
& quivered under lightning

bless all our monsters made & changed

bless everyone who looked at you, knew & looked away

Madness & Recovery

GRIEVING CEREMONY TO UNMAKE GIRLS

A bundle of ideas is holding your place.
You are not here. You never were.
This you, now, isn't real.
Watch yourself fade
leaving
grunting men face down
thrusting into empty beds.

THE TREES AT QUEEN & OSSINGTON CALL OUT

kneel
go to ground
calculate flight patterns.

Stretch the belly, take a little more
for glory-damned morning birds
flitting in the hospital parking lot.

No medicine
for early nests caught
in late snow.

VISITING HOURS

Who will care for her, our amnesiac pilot, stranded by oceanarium?

Noli timere so thin it comes out of her mouth as feathers.

If I threw her from the roof she'd float.

Ribcage unfurling, suspended in nimbus of numbers & light.

INVENTORY

we, the chemically shasted, slow-dance
without touching (the extras cost)

we did not feed our guides
                        who forgave us
our panicked inventories

we, the butterflies on Big Pharma's box
the cats that don't come in, the children
who won't go down at night

this is how we come to them
when they call us into our names
giving us purr & glow in our bones

              & somewhere, a brief sensation
                      a door's been shut
                            the fire set

SCARCITY IN THE FACE OF COMPASSION

it's not all going to work out
some decisions will be bad

no one ever survived on a belly full of praise

be flamboyant, a mistake

we're old news
giants have come before us
clearing the way
with huge hearts
& impeccable swish

rumour is they're on their way back
wearing their grandmothers' furs
their lashes caked with glitter

a new order is coming
where we are all ascendant
& must learn to share

where we are all sick
(just not at the same time)

the giants are here to empty
the hospitals, to compel
the breathless to get up
and walk, if you can't walk
shuffle, if you can't shuffle
crawl

don't you already know?
the momentum of any Queer Parade
saves more than just souls

THE TREES AT QUEEN & OSSINGTON WATCH

glory-damned morning birds slam
into windows under mid-Atlantic blue sky
colour of distance never arriving.

The trees keen, bioacoustic redeemers
doctors of unmediated loss teaching us

to diagnose rage & treat slap-panicked fear
in the bodies it animates.

New words roost in their branches
ask us to be cautious, to consider

we have no idea what it is to wake
in an acre of stone-rolled erasure.

Remind us that sometimes the moon
is big
    & orange
        & free for everybody.

The Monster's Been Made

COMPANY OF WATER

for mother who gave me a name then took it away
when she heard my in utero apologies

for my uninvited girl-body, silent & over-excited

for the bodies that did not behave, did not succeed
as growing human concerns but understood winter
& her gradations of ice

(you made me more patient with my sorry's
                gentler with the uninvited girl)

for the sentience that stayed afloat passing along grief
in cold water so that we would not forget

                the beached & our true sins against them
                how it was not enough that our prayers
                had the same bones

all of this for the crib-side visitor that only my brother saw

I wait

the name you held me in

                        a blessing

                                    that washes away

PROTECTIVE STORIES FOR CHILDREN IN THE 1970'S

Your mother walks in on you having a bath
berates you for not telling her about the birthmark
above your left hip, necessary information
in case something happened.

The nightly news says your body
will be locked in an abandoned refrigerator
or be found face down in a creek. Should you
survive into your teens there is an after-school special
about the PCP that will make you throw
yourself through a fifth story window.

The people who love you will suffer silently
around the wet bars in their finished basements.

The babysitter you have a crush on
will rug hook a mat with your initials in autumn colors.
Leave it quietly outside your parents' front door.

OUR GAME

Airplane passengers report bits of stars on wings.
Last sizzle cooling to ash. Captain announces
cabin will be sprayed with flame retardant
as a precaution.

In emergency lighting.
astral dust mites whisper:

Hush   Monster   Hush

Our Test:

Run fingers over wrist.
Dig into grizzle of tendons.

                    Nausea?

Yes.

Human?

                    Yes. Human.

HOME MOVIES

Mother is so thin.

How is she to get words in her mouth?

How is he to get them out?

She calls us sweetest, *squees* us with her toes
tiny assassins, we don't know them until they're on us.

Later: Small lithium powered family circles self-inflicted wound.

Now: Dance for the camera. Head down. Pent. We
could be anything.

ALL OVER ON WINTER HOLIDAYS

the curtains are open
full bodied ghosts drink boxed wine
                    (throat)

she is outside looking in
                    (feet)

pane of glass in window
                    (forehead)

she is inside looking out
                    (stomach)

reaching for a box-cutter or the medicine cabinet
                    (sweat under breasts)

her baffled face when the doctor asks;
where does she feel it   in her body?

THE HAZARDS OF PRAYER

I will not take three months of Percocet in one week.
Promise. On my soul & bowels.
I will live sharp-edged, teething.
You will show me, Brother, how to live through an emergency.
Don't sweet me with words like necessary or kind.
Teach martial duty, vigilance.
Because today they found a girl in a ravine
yesterday it was twenty-six at sea, their bodies
unbelonging to any country.

We will be careful. Avoid the words water & women.
But a question will bloat, pocketed in my cheek
or it will tire, slide down windpipe, be remembered
only as a burn
a small blue hurt.

MY BROTHER

Sing brother sing.
Mother bears down
pushes you out
& here you are
dog with torch in mouth
blood full of jump.

You chase a decade.
I run after you.
Rest.
I'm here now.
Drink as if you're free.

Alone, I sing *God*
he's done his job
done good
leave him be.

You lap young language.
In swollen sea your fur changes
to skin, the greys & almost blues
from your sonogram. Image courtesy
of our handmade satellite.

North of here
a watered country
full of fat Catholic salmon
ready to jump in your mouth.

MAIL FROM BRITISH COLUMBIA

The green pulse of your letter asks: am I still collecting cats & books?
How did we survive the dangers of Wash n' Go Perms in Canadian
    winters
& toxic shock syndrome from our tampons? Did we want to be
    revolutionaries
or the gun that went off in act three? Why no one in grade four
    noticed that you
came to school with your shirt on backwards, your eyes crusted shut?
Why our grade seven teacher told your parents you were a blue gumball
among pink gumballs?

Do I remember the glass ornaments our parents hung
in the seventies at Christmas time?

So fragile, they hurt in the box.

Life Now

(for Reg)

COLD WONDERS & OTHER MIRACLES

You put up with a bit of prayer as long as it comes with coffee & soup.
In your youth you were lost, shaggy and matted. Always sure you were
ready for a new run—to show us what it was to have four legs at mid-
night in a port city, to know the secret spot where boys go to jump.

You were nobody's bitch, but a sucker for a scratch behind the ears,
stuck between answers & commands: *sit, stay, be well, get up and walk.*

Burrs in your fur whisper questions. You see a small plane drop
leaflets for free ginger ale & the mad scramble of your boyhood
is on you like a fever.

I want your dreams to be of your wife, Betty
                                        who you will remember.

There were months where you wanted to die. Not wished to. Wanted.
But that has passed. You have a hospital bed with a curtain in a room
with three other men. An info sheet on scabies taped to the wall.
The last thing you remember is The Old Brewery Mission in 1970.
So your current circumstances seem great.

Is there lightness in absence? I want that for you.

The life you lived, a life of trying was a good life even if you don't
remember.

When I visit you tell me to reach out. Reach out. Find a frozen man's
hand.
If the wrist is chewed clean through, a dog's been at it. Laugh. Laugh.
One life in a pack isn't much. So laugh, say we're alike. Hard & happy.

                                   That it's ok to look at ourselves now.

HERE

I like my life now. I found my suicide note from seventeen years ago.
It was a thank you list.
Old habits are hard to break. I worry about loneliness, abandonment,
the future.
Sometimes I still repeat to myself: *in case of diminished capacity
refuse water*, as if I could hardwire it into my cerebellum.

But I like my life now.

FIGHT OR FLIGHT

Freeze.
How long can you hold your breath for?
Can you hurt someone if you have to?

        I knew you might be dying
         when I dreamed I coughed up
        3 of your sharp teeth.
        This was the week of Easter
        & transdermal pain meds.

Try flight. Complications may save you.
If this fails find your inner Jacob
& wrestle a lesser angel on the corner of Misery
& Fuck Up. Force a blessing.

Make sure it's transferable.

WHAT PARTY FAVOURS GO WITH GRIEF?

crown of elementary particles
around your head, holy ghost
licking your spine, whispering
"no more thirst, here's to your
good work, well done & good night"

flat ginger ale & lemon cough drops
could only do so much
& there will be no resurrection
through B12 shots
(although you claim otherwise)

I thought we would somehow escape
this part, that we were safe

you remind me of my Dad
stubborn as hell

your favourite word: *bullshit*

I picture you, gone ahead, shedding
the bullshit of being human, moving
with an easy confidence, drunk
on marigold petals, all your fears
(what you couldn't say out loud)
finally gone to bed

IN MEMORIAM

Death is the first surprise. The second is that the living continue
    to live, bright and precise,
untouched by the serrated edges of grief.

I have frost in my lungs. A slight breeze could kneecap me with
    loneliness.

But I am not bright and precise or alone. There are crowds of us.
We know each other by our bleached auras—a yellow grit
smelling of polyester sweat. Our best was not good enough.
We would give anything. We dream of being sunlight
in the bed sheets, keepers of final moments.

We wake at 3 in the morning and shuffle to greet the day
because there is no more sleep.
We are citizens of small worlds getting smaller,
light-seekers measuring each step
heart-bruised by the business of living.

FOSSILS FROM THE 6TH EXTINCTION WILL NOT BE FOUND

Check your windowsill.
I left king cans of Arizona Ice Tea
& smokes
Export A Gold.

Right now, I am a fisher
on dry land, running
wide with a net, looking back
to catch your eye.

When you aren't writing
you finger wooden beads
while staring out the window.

Your words on the page
single-celled organisms
evolving to replace us
never knowing we were here

or how you required the company
of rocks & straight vertical drops
into caves so deep your mother forgot you.

At your monument I will leave
a package tied with thin wire
& fine weather; full of teeth
bones, fur, a spoon—all you will need
to get back to the mountain.

Monuments

CHOKE

This is a curse covered in cum.
A protective spell for the entire population.

This is for you saying: shut up shut up shut the fuck up
put something with tits on the stage.

This is for the girl up there working for tips

.

& your friends' backslapping laughter.

This is her curse. Where it starts.

May you choke in the presence of XXX chromosomes
as your teeth chew through the back of your throat
& you gag for air.

Snap.

This is sound of your ribs cracking from kind strangers
who give you the Heimlich every time you try to speak.

THE DO-YOU-LIKE-ME-THEN-I-LIKE-YOU PANOPTICON

Little altars are everywhere; hordes
of attention from creeped gods
with backpacks full of Labatt's 50
fists full of crumpled five-dollar bills.
They can smell our *please-pick-me* recycled shame.

It's not nothing to know about this place
easy to see how a girl can feel
like a walking garbage can.
No coherent narrative here
in choosing one we burn ourselves
or someone else.
The altars have nothing to do with us
someone else's fetish.

We are forgotten in that we are not who we were.

This is a test
see, now I can say
are-you-hurt & tell-me-what-to-do.
This is just a visit.

We knew that our girl-bodies were knives
& we never once thought to slit their throats.

That's not nothing.

MONTREAL TO EDMONTON

You keep a butter knife and a porn mag under your bed. We do
   too much coke.
You pull out Miss December, whisper "God isn't fair" in my ear.
   I know.

Neighbors' alarms start beeping. This is the hour when desperate
   small dogs whine
to join their comrades in the street getting high off the melt.

This is the spring of dopamine spasms and spontaneous nose bleeds.
Next will be the summer with its careful clean needles and botched veins.
I leave on Labour Day with its frustrated airports and geographic cures.
To be fair (although life isn't) I loved you until October.

GIRL MEDICINE

Green-tipped knives in the sky sing Eukarya!
One gentle sinner swims in prophylactic
blue-scored sleep, edged with burnt oranges
yellows that hurt.

Then there are two.

Plant them when the knives turn to syringes.

Find a basement bedroom, before computers, ideally
a home that argues Avon vs Mary Kay.

Just this once let our medicine
be beautiful & without fuck up.

Care for them both when mother wishes one was sick.
Keep them Queer and sun-cupped, these two horsey girls
as eager to run into a barn fire as away from it.

CITY GIRL DISSOCIATION

Blue Hurts are historical
but redacted, fictional
by the time they know their names.

They approach the podium hesitant to lean in.
Amplification is dangerous, so they fold
themselves origami style into our DNA.

They are how we learned to leave our bodies
while staying in the room.
Left alone,
they are nervous creatures
& unlike us
will work together to save themselves.

They are two sides of a jagged cut
that make do, the threat of a pulse
combined with your sister's weight
and sureness,
hums you elbow to wrist,
puts you to bed in clean sheets,
says shush now,
here you are
in your body
not having gone away.

CONTENTS
(one box of loss)

dead pets
mountain air
modern revivalism —
          the hope that made her beg
ice water & blood oranges
transient divinities
baby teeth cleaned in kitchen kettle
compromised veins
72 lbs of a girl we failed

DIRECTIVE

Be one many great saviors.
Refuse & tidy words.

Be big, shared
sweet-sweet
even when air-drunk & under-touched.

Be gentle.
Patience is more than not causing harm.

Be prophetic witness
to the Holy Lonely. Lose your breath
& your knees when you see
how the unmothered forgive.

Run with your small story.
You have work to do:
forehead to open on coffee table
rusty nail to pierce through flip flop.
            Grow.
Change your mind over & over.
Your body is the problem. No.
It's your mouth.

You are a guest here. Of course it's painful.
Why wouldn't it be?

Say no when you have to.
Say no when you want to.
Have moments of faith that scare you.
Be horrified by your feelings.
If it helps, pay someone
to forgive your thoughts.

Let some god, any god, be your many-gendered lover.

This will be hard. You will have to learn
you are not a precarious product of salvation.
You are solid.

Pitch your body, tent in the switchgrass.
Listen for the others, young & old
crying loss in the field.
Help them bury the box at their feet.
Clean them up.
There is work to do.

MONUMENT

May you thrive in the coming crystal-booted biogenic future. May
you be prepared. Know your new muscles, the insect angle of
your arms. You are new. New Citizen of Grass. You will be speck
& function. There is cursive script all over you for someone else to
read. Amen your secrets. Amen your hard joys, holy & humbled,
gone tight when you understood The Terror of the Glory. You will
have one hundred nameless daughters who will remember the
girls & women that we forgot. You will all be Citizens of Grass,
saying each woman & girl's name simultaneously, slowly, round
after round, harmonies of loss. As you finish a jewel will appear
on your tongue. Spit it out. Begin again. These stones will be sent
to what is left of their families. Some will hold them in confusion.
Some will weep. Some will come yearly to collect. Some will come
screaming that you mangled their names, that they have no business on your tongue *so shut your mouth shut your mouth shut your
mouth*. They will be right. You will be silent & still. Your organs
will slow with yearning. The songs of your daughters will cause
crystals to grow inside you, reaching out, metabolizing into angles
& facets. Thousands of years from now, standing alone in the
sand, your sharp lines & clean edges will sing all of their names
at once. The vibrations will bounce off magnetic fields, ping off of
old satellites (tired dogs) circling the earth. The transmission will
travel further than any man ever imagined.

This is loss.
This is love.
This is remembering.

ECHO TO HER SISTERS

I loved a mirrored man
body a warm box of milk
day away from turning

for which there is no cure no cure no cure
hope is not a plan
we will all go dark shortly

   be careful sisters
   they'll try to sleep inside you
   dump a virus in your blood
   an ID chip in your neck
   bright smiles of science
   will weaponize your name

my snipped collar will be found
on a dancefloor full of dead soundtracks

on the download know I was proud
of your unsupervised hiss & static
rough edits from an eighties mixtape

pure radio magic

O child Anarchia, infinite promise
infinite carelessness
I listen, listen in the night
Ursula K. LeGuin, The Dispossesed

GUIDE OUR MOUTHS DEAR URSULA

What we do, we do full of inflammation.
We are infection.
Our damp voices slipped into Girl-Bodies
left to burn into women. We diagnose ourselves
sniff fingers (church incense, polyester).
Run same fingers over teeth. Taste Middle Earth.
Lord of the Rings Pussy.

Yes Ursula we do we do we do.

This human place hunts us. Give us a story to tell our lives.
How the trees keep faith, throwing birds into the sky
& we play with our DNA scraping cells onto slides
crisping our way closer to you.

Ursula, are you crying?

Maybe you can't hear us. We are small, long gone.
Maybe you forgot us. No matter, no mother, new mother.
Greetings! We are your deep in the night children
even a tree with faith cannot know if we keep our promises.
We are your obstinate birds Ursula, nesting in harsh places.

WHEN THERE IS NOTHING LEFT IN THE GROUND

The iron in our blood will demagnetize
our credit cards, key fobs & transit passes.
We will be identified as hungry underperforming
flesh platforms.

In the long absence we will turn our pink irradiated
bellies towards the muck of the sun until we shake
& spew, methane from our bodies will spark
the barbed-wire, burning the air.

A snot rocket from a sneeze will shoot forward
DNA embedded with childhood ritual crossed
with Roman Catholic rigour.

> One possible future: we are born
> never able to feel safe while asleep.

A SISTER TO ECHO

no more drinking from toilets
with fast tongues, glittering silver teeth
no sitting pretty begging for scraps

we were loved ugly, come round the sun
decommissioned needful things, unsure
if our barks were broken or lost in transit

all our sisters below us, mouths full
of wet sand, mothering stillness
clean in their work

sound waves in their DNA, a signal to look up
look up   our bodies glow
bright in the night sky   bark arrives in throat

they know us, they know us by the shared smell
in our bellies

                         fine weather & blue hurt

NEW NOAH BEGINS HER LESSONS

Spark
be filament at bottom of sea
know the prehistoric creatures
who chose darkness.

Find words
for 3 months of rain
that falls in 4 days.

Suppress
the urge to build
a boat for animals
caught in human disasters.

Sit
with the rabbit who broke
her back by kicking
her legs in fear—
do the math.
Where does her allotment of sunlight go?

How does she tally in the sum of our extinctions?

The Book of Blue Hurts

*

My prescriptions launch themselves from my bedside table,
    leaving one clear directive:
Flush Us.

I am confident the fish in Lake Ontario are relaxed & do not suffer
    from psychosis.

Enjoy the rainbow trout.

*

COMMITMENT

I trade you small pot of light
for key that sticks in door.

Our worst nights, coin toss
burn house or bed down.

Wool-drunk moths in sock drawer
judge our quiet violence and dime-bag sentiment

but then we have an early evening
you mostly sober, me mostly clean

thinking of every possible animal afterlife.

Prescription sleeping pills smuggle
us into sleep, where we are strangers.

Cross the street to avoid each other.
Drowning girl can't climb
on another body, call it shore.

*

Looking out the window on a grey winter day, my head snaps
   violently upwards.

I am filled with the nausea of yellows & pinks & questions I don't
   want in my brain.

> Is this you trying to make up for what happened
> with your children?
> Is this me letting you?

My head snaps down, thoughts expunged.

Only chiropractors will benefit here.

*

DEAR JUDAS TREE

How about making it hurt?
Don't worry the regular folk.
I'm here to bargain.

I've got a man-boy with me
septic with lonely.
The thickness in his belly
a failed negotiation.
Can you help?

The best I could was packaged
intentions, shining ourselves
like money in the sun
all ohs on the half breath, trying
for a life north of the body.
Burying it in beginner's junk.

If you give him a Throwback Thursday
where his sister's still alive
& his adult sons don't hate him.
I'll set my swing on your branch. Stay.

You can castigate, immolate, revelate.
I'll swallow the wondersick
at the back of my mouth, answer
I like it just fine.

Judas, help a girl make a thin gift last.

*

You & I dream in unison of our mothers practicing at
Hammond Organs, school projects on the Ozone hole,
note on grocer bulletin board:

grey & white found, south parking lot

Sorry for your loss

We surface too quickly, divers with the bends

This feeling that can't be benzo'ed, exercised or fucked away

*

SMALL PURSE OF LIGHT

What's being right worth to you?
Can we admit we fucked up?

Let's be humble. Flight
is not freedom & the facility
for old wounds is closed.

Sometimes we fail each other
                                on purpose.

Let's be happy, no more Christmases
or Father's Days.

Let's be shit-bag corny in our devotion,
whisper in the dark, "it's ok baby, everything's ok".

Let's be fearless, undefended
wet-in-the-nest new
a relentless beginning
that turns white noise green.

Baby let's swim in unslit skin.

                    We're good in the water.

*

Creatures of habit, we give when it doesn't cost. Sneak
each other's browser histories.
Like what we shouldn't.

Our love is a minor disaster.

But if the good journey is a myth, you prove that the decent one is not.

*

Mythos

Fragments from the Biophilia Codex

MARGINALIA

(found hand-written in first edition of The Book of Common Prayer)

I have a tongue that spins lichens
coaxes a fox from her winter den
I am pessimist & possibility.
Drag a fir tree behind me to dust
away my footprints but those particles
rise, tell their own story:
"Bless no more Bishop, even the wicked need a place to rest."

IN THEIR NAMES
(liturgical)

Your lazy feathered future is welcome here
We will show you how to be uncomplicated star shapes
The guests you need walk out the door
Your hope they die   arrive safely

> *but don't you deserve it*
> *& aren't you a fool*
> *standing by yourself*
> *in a house full of empty chairs*

We too have been far from what we are for

The person who loves you hasn't been born yet

> *we've locked the uncles in the basement*
> *their voices, sly with shine, kept asking*
> *how free did we want to be?*
> *So we broke their fingers*

Your crow jealous heart is safe here

We too are for the hard work of caring & when hurt
double-down, try to please
                    someone

                    anyone

each morning a humiliation

So put on your sinner's grin & a festival crown

Invite us in

soul-illumined   love-wrecked

we will all meet at the common grave

UNIDENTIFIED CONGREGANT
(ephemera)

hiding in groves, our proximity
to hanging fruit bakes it on the tree

eat without reason or want

we are the generation that trickled
in after The Blame, always empty or too full

we feel relief when we lose consciousness
bodies fall, shatter on impact
leave an ice patch, sour the soil

Glaucous stomps the ground
drumming shallow roots into
a backwards crawl, where neck deep
in water we find a boat in our breast pocket
& women sell sailing winds knotted in handkerchiefs

FATHER OF MICROBIOLOGY
Leeuwenhoek & his microscope (sermon by Glaucous)

Buries his second child
grieves

       makes a tube from tin
fills it with whiskers of glass

Buries his third child
grieves

       makes a tube of silver
& finer filaments
peers through it
(so close so close so close)

Buries his fourth child
grieves

       makes a tube of copper
fits it with his finest lens
scrapes a glass plate
along the inside
of his mouth
inserts under lens
peers through it
there
small, struggling
stains them with saffron
sees them clear
furiously peddling
baptizes them *Animicules*

Here we teem with painful abundance

NEW FUTURE @ PRAYER
(provenance unknown)

sits on back porch
fist in her mouth
tries to boil the water

bits of him crumble
by the hour
she & her brother are gasoline
& used bullets
they are a sweet abrasion
a mother's tongue

incapable of apology

he used to be humble medicine
in a bucket of water
(in case she caught fire)

if he will be a banjo
she will strap him to her back
busk big tent revivals

this time they will know better
refuse blessings & prayers

accept only matches

COMMUNAL RESPONSE, BOOK OF COMMON PRAYER & REFLECTION

we stumble in, plastic bottles in hands
vape pens in pockets
unable to look each other in the eye

our weight buckles the floor
we are very late
come for the microbes in holy water
—Leeuwenhoek's Animicules

when The Great Eye is Glaucous
we must love what we cannot see

*

a moment of silence please
for Nordic countries mourning glacier death

a plaque in Iceland reads:
we know what is happening, what needs to be done
only you will know if we did it

in our church moments of silence pile up
tongues-thick shamed slugs at back of throats

*

our continent traffics in unwanted bodies
& crashes our endocrine systems, we lack
capacity to be moth spun, watch spiders
worry over prayer books for their cousins
—New Arachnauts, nano-satellites in space

we pray for genetic anomalies & ascension
desperate to ignore the truth

we will never be judged

which is another truth

don't we feel relief?

NEW FUTURE TO GLAUCOUS

(transcribed by unknown congregant)

I gave you one simple job;
keep your time piece rusted.

Well it ticked last night.

Thin, slippery babies performed their own
C-sections as mothers slept. I had to blanket
the hemispheres with aurora borealis fireworks
to cover their cries & distract museum curators
from noticing their avian specimens twitch
as they woke in tiny glass compartments.

Were you there for their last raspy confessions?

I traded our Gift of Homing by Sight to stop
the clock. Last time I checked help was a 2 degree
roll-back that is never coming.

Explain that to them, Lord of Telescopes.

ON GLAUCOUS
(New Future speaks/canonical dissent/unverified origin)

My brother is a long collision, a crucible
a fevered biophiliac & a pain in the ass.
He fathers theology, parents nothing
skips rope with gravity, curious about chaos.
Leaves me to clean up the mess.

It was all of you gave him superhuman powers.

We were nothing. Siblings who hadn't earned a story.

He tells us all to find worship in the quieter places,
drop of moisture on stalactite, intricate dirt pathways
of fungi before they bloom.

You are tremors in uneven deceleration.
You are the authors, why do you still call for him?
Be careful with your own story. Whatever he tells you
radiance is not a birthright.

LETTER FROM GLAUCOUS TO NEW FUTURE
(annotated Book of Reflection)

I spent too much time in the sky searching for a celestial crawlspace
(I had no business being there, our father, a planet that ate his own stars).
I thought the common grave would yield...Hoped if I stayed away
you wouldn't notice the changes, law of diminishing returns.

I try to move as little as possible. Spend days (years?) thinking
about how our mother covered her face with a blanket of pollen
so we wouldn't know her. Left us in a cave with bees to feed us.
In-utero we pretended to be ravens swimming round each other.
You came out first: quadruped. Me second: biped. You telling
me I was made from your leftovers. Me screaming. You laughing.
Me screaming harder for you to take it back, then...a mouth full
of bees buzzing me into a lulled silence. You licking honey from
my face.

Sometimes I think we are back. Two birds fluttering to an absent
mother's heartbeat. Together, content, unfinished

FROM OBJECTS OF PRAYER TO A BEDTIME STORY
(unknown congregant, folklore)

When Glaucous died, New Future wretched an ocean. It rained fish.
She picked her brother up in her mouth and started an Infinity Loop.
Perpetual motion far from Elysium where they dared each other to cross
worlds; children in one, gods in another.

After the fields failed, relics were good barter. She watched
The Glaucous Journals go for three bags of flour. The pages
were scribbled with the observations of an amateur astronomer.

LETTER
(provenance unknown, found in Isafjordur cave)

You won't get through on the dream-line. I medicate it. But if you come
I want to know. I'll wrap my house in fish skin, set out tealights.
Look for the flicker.

I stopped walking when there was nothing left of you to carry. It took
a long time. They don't know us anymore. I live by the water.
I walk upright. I am settled here in this patch of solution, great
        experiment
by careful new beings.

I found the stone whistle you left for me, am learning to read the rocks—
so full of your stupid abundance.

ACKNOWLEDGMENTS

I am a settler on the lands of the Mississaugas of the Credit, of the Anishnabeg, the Chippewa, the Haundenosaunee, and the Wendat peoples. They are the true stewards of this land for which I am grateful.

Thank you to the editorial teams at these literary journals for providing a home for pieces from Mouthful of Bees:

Mail from British Columbia, My Brother, Home Movies, All Over on Winter Holidays, **Contemporary Verse 2**

The Hazards of Prayer, Inventory, Transmission, A Beautiful Math, **SubTerrain**

Monument **Geez**, Poetics of Resistance

City Girl Dissociation, **The Dalhousie Review**

Last Boy Astronaut, Girl Medicine, Echo to her Sisters, **The Malahat Review**

Equanimity, Fossils for the Sixth Extinction will not be Found, The Pack Animal Tarot, **Qwerty**

Song to Call a Body Home, **Prairie Fire**

New Future @ Prayer, Letter from Glaucous to New Future, Letter from New Future, **Fourth River Literary Journal**

Panopticon, Montreal to Edmonton, **Outlook Springs**

Commitment, **SWIMM**

Thank you to the Canada Council for the Arts for supporting this project.

Thank you to griffin epstein and bryan depuy, who worked to turn "Fragments from the Biophilia Codex" into an interactive digital experience. Our work on this specific section can be experienced here: https://whosewoods.org/biophilia/

I had the privilege of spending time in residence at the Leighton Colony at the Banff Centre, Hospitalfield House in Scotland and Westfjords in Iceland. All of which offered me adventures along with the opportunity for peace and contemplation

Thank you to my Mom, Doris Quinn and to my brothers and sisters: Maureen, Eileen, Michael, Kevin and Dennis (and their amazing partners) for their love and acceptance.

Thank you to Hume Cronyn and Chris Beyers, my writing group compatriots and to Lorne Tugg, for helping me keep it all together. Thank you, Kristyn Dunnion, for being a bridge between worlds, to David Rigsbee for his valuable feedback and Robert Barlow for precious morning coffee and the gift of time.

I can't accurately capture the names of everyone who offers me their support and love, so to all my friends and colleagues, I hope you know to insert your names here.

Lastly, thank you to everyone in my sober community who saved my life then helped me learn how to actually have a life.

Shannon Quinn is the author of two previous poetry collections: *Nightlight for Children of Insomniacs* (Mansfield Press) and *Questions for Wolf* (Thistledown Press). Quinn worked for CBC Radio in Iqaluit, Thunder Bay, Toronto and Ottawa as an associate producer before changing careers. She now lives in Toronto, Dish with One Spoon Territory, where she is proud to provide and use mental health and addiction services.